The rapid growth of academic literature in the field of economics has posed serious problems for both students and teachers of the subject. The latter find it difficult to keep pace with more than a few areas of their subject, so that an inevitable trend towards specialism emerges. The student quickly loses perspective as the maze of theories and models grows and the discipline accommodates an increasing amount of quantitative techniques.

'Macmillan Studies in Economics' is a new series which sets out to provide the student with short, reasonably critical surveys of the developments within the various specialist areas of theoretical and applied economics. At the same time, the studies aim to form an integrated series so that, seen as a whole, they supply a balanced overview of the subject of economics. The emphasis in each study is upon recent work, but each topic will generally be placed in a historical context so that the reader may see the logical development of thought through time. Selected bibliographies are provided to guide readers to more extensive works. Each study aims at a brief treatment of the salient problems in order to avoid clouding the issues in detailed argument. Nonetheless, the texts are largely self-contained, and presume only that the student has some knowledge of elementary microeconomics and macroeconomics.

Mathematical exposition has been adopted only where necessary. Some recent developments in economics are not readily comprehensible without some mathematics and statistics, and quantitative approaches also serve to shorten what would otherwise be lengthy and involved arguments. Where authors have found it necessary to introduce mathematical techniques, these techniques have been kept to a minimum. The emphasis is upon the economics, and not upon the quantitative methods. Later studies in the series will provide analyses of the links between quantitative methods, in particular econometrics, and economic analysis.

MACMILLAN STUDIES IN ECONOMICS

General Editors: D. C. ROWAN and G. R. FISHER

Executive Editor: D. W. PEARCE

Published

John Burton: WAGE INFLATION
Miles Fleming: MONETARY THEORY
C. J. Hawkins: THEORY OF THE FIRM
C. J. Hawkins and D. W. Pearce: CAPITAL INVESTMENT APPRAISAL
David F. Heathfield: PRODUCTION FUNCTIONS
Dudley Jackson: POVERTY
P. N. Junankar: INVESTMENT: THEORIES AND EVIDENCE
J. E. King: LABOUR ECONOMICS
J. A. Kregel: THE THEORY OF ECONOMIC GROWTH
George McKenzie: THE MONETARY THEORY OF INTERNATIONAL TRADE
S. K. Nath: A PERSPECTIVE OF WELFARE ECONOMICS
D. W. Pearce: COST-BENEFIT ANALYSIS
Maurice Peston: PUBLIC GOODS AND THE PUBLIC SECTOR
David Robertson: INTERNATIONAL TRADE POLICY
Charles K. Rowley: ANTITRUST AND ECONOMIC EFFICIENCY
C. H. Sharp: TRANSPORT ECONOMICS
G. K. Shaw: FISCAL POLICY
R. Shone: THE PURE THEORY OF INTERNATIONAL TRADE
Frank J. B. Stilwell: REGIONAL ECONOMIC POLICY
John Vaizey: THE ECONOMICS OF EDUCATION
Peter A. Victor: ECONOMICS OF POLLUTION
Grahame Walshe: INTERNATIONAL MONETARY REFORM
E. Roy Weintraub: GENERAL EQUILIBRIUM THEORY

Forthcoming

G. Denton: ECONOMICS OF INDICATIVE PLANNING
J. A. Kregel: THEORY OF CAPITAL
Richard Lecomber: ECONOMIC GROWTH AND ENVIRONMENTAL QUALITY
D. Mayston: THE IDEA OF SOCIAL CHOICE
Simon Mohan: RADICAL ECONOMICS
B. Morgan: MONETARISM AND KEYNESIANISM
Christopher Nash: PUBLIC *v.* PRIVATE TRANSPORT
A. Peaker: BRITISH ECONOMIC GROWTH SINCE 1945
F. Pennance: HOUSING ECONOMICS
Nicholas Rau: TRADE CYCLES: THEORY AND EVIDENCE
M. Stabler: AGRICULTURAL ECONOMICS
E. Roy Weintraub: THE ECONOMICS OF CONFLICT AND CO-OPERATION
J. Wiseman: PRICING PROBLEMS OF THE NATIONALISED INDUSTRIES

General Equilibrium Theory

E. ROY WEINTRAUB
Associate Professor of Economics, Duke University

Macmillan

First published 1974 by
THE MACMILLAN PRESS LTD
London and Basingstoke
Associated companies in New York Dublin
Melbourne Johannesburg and Madras

SBN 333 14460 0

Printed in Great Britain by
THE ANCHOR PRESS LTD
Tiptree, Essex

Contents

Preface and Acknowledgements

This monograph is addressed primarily to undergraduate economics students having some conventional familiarity with basic university mathematics. It is the author's belief that the complicated technical façade of general equilibrium theory has only served to frighten away students who are perfectly able to grasp the problems, the gist of the analysis, and the conclusions. After all, few of us have mastered the engineering details of the internal combustion engine, yet most of us have little trouble purchasing an automobile.

General equilibrium analysis is at the very centre of economic theory. International trade, labour economics, public finance, monetary theory, industrial organisation, etc. have all been enriched and aided by past work in general equilibrium theory.

Yet despite the centrality of their concerns, theorists have been unusually defensive about their intellectual preoccupation, since their interest usually stigmatised them as 'mathematical types with their heads in the clouds', who had nothing to contribute to practical matters.

I believe, however, that students today are able to grasp the conceptual framework of theories that their mentors abhorred for reasons of excessive symbolism. It has come to pass, as in so many other difficult subjects, that yesterday's research problem is a part of today's basic education. It is for this reason that Chapters 5 and 6, which are concerned with current controversies, have been included. This framework reflects my opinion that the micro–macro relationship via general equilibrium theory is too important to remain primarily a subject for postgraduate study.

The monograph itself was conceived in the U.K. and born in the U.S., and I have benefited from spirited conversation with colleagues and friends on both sides of the Atlantic. I spent academic year 1971–72 at the University of Bristol, and Professor Miles Fleming, Mr David Collard, Mr Anthony Brewer, and Mr Michael Wickens were an enormous help in shaping the views presented here. At Duke University I have been fortunate in having an exuberant collaboration with Professor Dan Graham. Professors Martin Bronfenbrenner, Marjorie McElroy, and Tom Havrilesky at Duke read and commented on a preliminary version of this manuscript, as did my personal editors Paul Davidson and Sidney Weintraub.

Miss Katie Frye, who typed the manuscript, has shown great patience in dealing with my impatience.

Finally, my wife Margaret, whose confidence in this project and its author continue to mean so much, points out that the only appropriate dedication is 'to Matthew, a little book for a little boy'.

E R W

1 Introduction

SYSTEMS

In the past several years, individual scholars in diverse disciplines have begun to use a common language to describe and analyse problems [1]. It has become evident that, while all fields of enquiry are not reducible to one another in the sense of a unified science, there are various ideas, concepts, and tools which have applicability in studies as separated as economic development and molecular biology, cybernetics and the law [1, 2].

General systems theory can be said to provide a set of common concepts by which problems sometimes thought to be separate may be recognised as similar. The crux of general systems theory is that certain notions, like system, parameter, equilibrium, state, stability, and control are used to describe situations in many fields of study. A biologist may speak of a living organism as a set of mutually related systems (e.g. locomotor, respiratory) hierarchically arranged, with various forms of feedback designed to control or mitigate pathological behaviour. A management theorist might speak of a factory as a complex of systems organised to attain certain goals, the attainment of which requires an information network to monitor unstable patterns, report them, and facilitate their control. And like Molière's gentleman, economists too have been speaking 'systems' for many years without realising the fact [3].

One aim of general systems theory might be to identify systems concepts in various areas and extract them from their contexts to provide an abstract model of a general system about which theorems could be proved; these theorems would then be applicable to biology, psychology, economics, cybernetics, the law, etc. Such a programme would be similar to the mathematician's search for common structure. Sets of transformations of plane objects (like the rotations of a square) and sets of polynomials have a structural similarity; they both form what mathematicians call a group. Proving propositions about groups eliminates the need to prove separate theorems for rotations and polynomials. At the present time this potential of general systems theory is unrealised. So far, little is known about general systems that was not known previously about particular systems [4].

The value of general systems theory, then, is not as a universal mathematical structure but rather as a diagnostic tool. For example, it has been suggested that where an equilibrium notion exists in a discipline, one ought also to look for those mechanisms which move disequilibrium states to equilibrium ones. General systems theory has been quite fruitful in the intuitive end of science, hypothesis-creation, and rather less successful in normal science, or the work of falsification of hypotheses.

Since it will be argued shortly that general equilibrium theory, and much of economics, is concerned with the analysis of systems, it will serve some purpose to set out various systems concepts. At the very least, if it is shown that there are systems attributes missing in an economic model, incorporation of such attributes may dispel some objections to the model.

Alternatively, if two economic models of the same phenomenon are both supported by tests of their conclusions, but one is unable (or is too rigidly delineated) to deal with questions which arise routinely in *any* systems context, then that model might be judged less worthy of study, for it could generate fewer testable conclusions.

SYSTEMS DEFINITIONS

A system may be defined as a pair of sets, together with a rule which specifies the relationship between subsets of the first set and subsets of the second set [2]. Intuitively, the first set consists of inputs, and the second of outputs, and the rule defines the relationship of inputs to outputs. If the presence of some set of objects entails a specific conjunction of inputs with outputs, that set is called a *state* of the system. For example, consider the system of a light switch and a lamp. The inputs of the system are the two switch positions, 'up' or 'down'; the outputs are 'light on' and 'light off.' Suppose a state of the system is determined by the position of the switch. A parameter might be the 'on' position of a master switch.

An *equilibrium state* of the system is a state such that, if the system is in that state, the rules which transform inputs to outputs ensure that that state will be maintained. A *stable equilibrium* (state) is a state such that, if the system is not in that state, the rules are such that the equilibrium will be achieved. For example, suppose that in the above system when the switch is up, the light is on. This is an equilibrium state since there are no rules which change the switch position. Similarly the down position determines an equilibrium state. If a photosensitive device is linked to the existing system, and this device responds to light by moving the switch down, then the down–off position is a stable equilibrium state of the system. The photosensitive device is a *control* mechanism which has the information inputs of 'light', and 'dark', and the outputs of 'switch down' and 'do nothing'.

A PARTIAL EQUILIBRIUM MODEL

To see that these systems concepts can be useful in analysing economic phenomena, consider the problem of determining the price at which a particular commodity will sell. Assume that the commodity is sold in a perfectly competitive market so that, from the behaviour of individual consumers and producers, there is a market demand curve and a market supply curve.

Further, assume that the market is so organised that an excess demand at some price entails an increase in price, and a negative excess demand (excess supply) entails a fall in price. If the market can be thought of as a system, a state of the system is a particular price. The Walrasian mechanism states that excess demand (supply) moves price up (down); in the systems sense, prices are inputs and prices are outputs. Hence an equilibrium price is one such that there is neither positive nor negative excess demand; excess demand is thus zero, so an equilibrium price is one such that demand quantities equal supply quantities.

Is such an equilibrium stable? Consider the diagrams in Fig. 1.

In Fig. 1a, at prices above p_e excess demand is negative so price falls, and at prices below p_e excess demand is positive so price rises. At any disequilibrium price, there is a mechanism which ensures that equilibrium will be attained. The equilibrium state is stable. In Fig. 1b, at prices above (below) p_e,

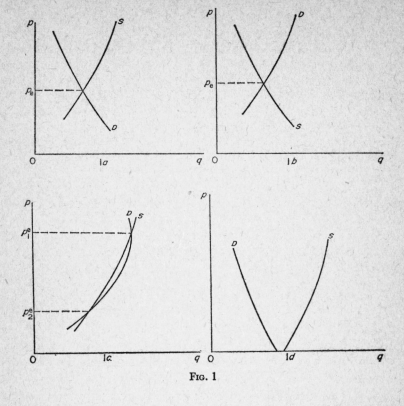

Fig. 1

excess demand is positive (negative) so price rises (falls). This equilibrium is unstable. In Fig. 1c it is obvious that p^e_1 is a stable equilibrium, and p^e_2 is an unstable equilibrium. In Fig. 1d a positive equilibrium price does not even exist.

Parameters for this system include those items whose change entails a changed output for a given input. If consumers' income increases, for instance, the demand curve might shift, entailing a different excess demand at any price, and thus a different equilibrium.

From this example it ought to be clear that a partial equilibrium model of a single market is a system in the sense of general systems theory although it is, of course, a very simple system. Nonetheless the systems approach to general equilibrium analysis may be introduced by examination of this simple market model.

For example, Figs. 1a–1d yield results of stable unique equilibrium, unstable unique equilibrium, multiple equilibria, and non-existence of equilibrium. What is at issue here are three distinct questions:

(1) Given an arbitrary system, does an equilibrium exist? (The existence problem.)

(2) Given a system for which an equilibrium exists, is that equilibrium unique? (The uniqueness problem.)

(3) Given an equilibrium state of a system, is that equilibrium stable? (The stability problem.)

In the single market model, the existence problem can be broached by asking for the conditions on consumer and producer behaviour which ensure that demand and supply curves intersect. The uniqueness problem may be framed in terms of the smoothness[1] or convexity[2] of the excess demand curve. The stability question clearly depends on the relationship between the slopes of the demand and supply curves.

If $E(p) = D(p) - S(p)$ is the excess demand function, where $D(p)$ and $S(p)$ are the demand and supply functions respectively, then rewriting Figs. 1a–1d in terms of $E(p)$ yields Fig. 2.

Geometrically, if $E(p)$ crosses the vertical (p) axis exactly n times, n equilibria exist, and if the slope of $E(p)$ at an equilibrium is negative, then that equilibrium is stable.

The slope of the excess demand curve, at p_e, is the derivative of $E(p)$ with respect to p, so the condition that an equilibrium p_e be stable is that

$$\frac{dE(p)}{dp}\bigg|_{p_e} < 0.$$

The condition that an equilibrium exist is that there exist a $p_e > 0$ such that $E(p_e) = 0$; if, for any $p \neq p_e$, $E(p) \neq 0$, then p_e is a unique equilibrium.

An implication of this argument is that, in an exchange situation where $S(p) = $ constant, the stability of equilibrium depends on the slope of the demand curve; since

$$\frac{dE(p)}{dp} = \frac{dD(p)}{dp} - \frac{dS(p)}{dp} = \frac{dD(p)}{dp},$$

the equilibrium will be unstable only if the demand curve is upward sloping at the equilibrium point.

[1] 'Smoothness' of a function generally refers to its continuity.

[2] A function is *convex* if a straight line drawn through any two points in its graph lies wholly on or above that graph.

13

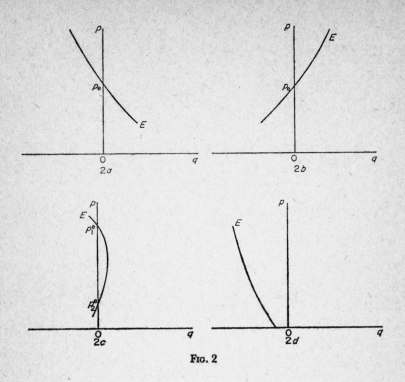

FIG. 2

THE GENERAL EQUILIBRIUM PROBLEM

Consider an extension of the above problem, in which there are three markets and thus three excess demand functions; since the demand for any good depends on its own price *and* the price of other goods, the excess demand for good two say, E_2, will depend on p_1, p_2, p_3 so that $E_2 = E_2(p_1, p_2, p_3)$. Similarly $E_1 = E_1(p_1, p_2, p_3)$ and $E_3 = E_3(p_1, p_2, p_3)$.

If the Walrasian adjustment rule is posited, so that E_i positive entails that p_i increases, the following questions arise:

(1) Does there exist a set, or vector, of prices (p_1^e, p_2^e, p_3^e) such that $E_i(p_1^e, p_2^e, p_3^e) = 0$ for $i = 1, 2, 3$?

(2) Is such a vector unique? and

(3) Is such an equilibrium vector stable?

The last question is especially intriguing: suppose that market 1 is in equilibrium, market 2 is not, and in market 3, $E_3(p_1, p_2, p_3) > 0$, so that excess demand prevails there. The adjustment rule increases the price, p_3, of the third good. But as p_3 changes, E_1 and E_2 will necessarily change since E_1 and E_2 depend on

14

p_3. Say that $E_1 < 0$, then p_1 falls; but E_3 depends on p_1, so E_3 changes, inducing movement in p_3, etc. Will the multi-market system ever settle down? What attributes of the market ensure that equilibrium will be attained?

Speaking broadly, general equilibrium theory in economics views the economy as a vast system of mutually interdependent markets. General equilibrium theory seeks to analyse the economy from the microeconomic viewpoint of individual markets considered simultaneously.

It should be clear that since general equilibrium theory deals with systems of markets, it has the flavour of a general systems study. What distinguishes, in a systems context, a partial equilibrium model from a general equilibrium model is that in the former prices in all other markets are parameters (or exogeneous variables) while in the latter they are state variables (or endogeneous variables) [4].

What is not so often recognised, in a first attempt to read the economics literature, is that macroeconomics and general equilibrium analysis are likewise intertwined [5]. Viewing the economic system in aggregative terms, a state of the system may be defined for example by a configuration of national income, consumption expenditures, investment outlays, employment, and average wage and price levels. The Keynesian system would specify particular relationships among these variables, and it would focus on certain adjustment mechanisms; propensities to consume out of various types of income might be parameters, and the money supply might be a control variable under the thumb of the central bank; this control mechanism may take price level movements to be information inputs [6].

The interrelationship of general equilibrium theory and macroeconomics is even more specific. In a real sense, macroeconomics *is* general equilibrium theory with some of the many markets grouped together for expositional clarity and convenience. In a general equilibrium schema of about 80,000 markets describing the behaviour of all prices in an economy, perhaps the first 40,000 markets are for consumer goods, the next 20,000 for capital goods, with 10,000 markets for labour services, 10,000 for financial assets, and a few for money. Combining markets for similar goods there is 'merely' the problem of five markets: consumer goods, investment goods, labour services, financial assets, and money.

Viewed in such a manner a general equilibrium system is simply a totally disaggregated macroeconomic model.

A MICRO–MACRO INTERFACE

If a general equilibrium system is a complete microeconomic model, and simultaneously a detailed approach to macroeconomics, why study anything in economics *except* general equilibrium systems? The answer should be obvious – they are exceedingly difficult to analyse, something succeeding chapters will make clear. The complexity of real-world markets almost entails that no two of them are exactly alike; the analyst must thus ignore particular structures when he views them as only two of n markets in a general system. While it is not logically necessary to put aside consideration of particular market characteristics in a general equilibrium study, their inclusion entails monumental analytical difficulties.[1] Until the economist's tools are as powerful as his intuitions, general equilibrium theory must play a different role. What might this be?

First, one might study general equilibrium systems for their own sake. The theory certainly provides a very general view of economic interrelationships since the information which has been abstracted from each particular market is completely basic. On this view one works at a formal level to see whether minimal restrictions on the system will generate some testable conclusions. Indeed, it is remarkable that some economically meaningful assumptions ensure the existence of an equilibrium price vector; further, this price vector can be shown to possess various optimality properties.

If it is believed that the world is not in equilibrium, and sub-optimality is omnipresent, then it is of interest to ask just what particular market characteristics disturb the results. If for example external diseconomies entail non-optimal solutions, one is dealing with a particular real phenomenon, and one can then assess its practical importance [7].

Second, one might study general equilibrium systems in order to resolve macroeconomic problems. If, given two aggregative theories (both of which are consistent with the

---

[1] For example, is the automobile market just like the market for pigs?

statistical data[1]), but one can be shown to have closer links to individual optimising behaviour, that theory might be considered more nearly correct since it has a better grounding in the larger body of economic knowledge. Viewed another way, if of two macroeconomic theories one presumed a view of individual demand curves at variance with market facts, that theory would be a candidate for rejection.

In practice, these two approaches to general equilibrium theory often are intermingled in any particular study; at the present time, perhaps, the latter view is the more dominant one. As the Keynes–Classics debate has been reopened, there are two, or three, possibly conflicting macroeconomic theories [6, 8]. Appeals are currently being made to general equilibrium theory to adjudicate the rival positions [9]. Similarly recent controversies in capital theory trace some of their roots to the microeconomic foundations of economics, particularly general equilibrium theory [10]. And although various writers protest that general equilibrium theory as currently constituted fails to answer such important questions because of its airy and abstract nature, others have answered this criticism by producing general equilibrium systems sufficiently flexible, and rich in testable conclusions, for that theory to play a part in the controversies.

ATTRIBUTES OF THE THEORY

Consequently it is possible at this time to identify various elements that should be present in a general equilibrium model, if such a model is to be used in the several ways suggested above. The model should be based, quite explicitly, on the existing theories of individual behaviour; that is, it should be built on those models of consumer behaviour and production theory most likely to command support. This analytical base, with its assumptions as weak as can be devised, can be taken as the best current first approximation to the facts of multi-market behaviour.

Since it is even simpler to phrase market issues in an exchange (non-production) framework, one's studies might well begin with an analysis of barter transactions implicit in a

[1] In the sense that each has certain testable conclusions, and neither is refuted by empirical tests of those conclusions.

17

market-oriented economic system. If no results of interest can be proved for this rudimentary framework, then there is little hope one can establish basic theorems as more complicated structures are introduced.

Yet if results can be established, and it is felt that general equilibrium theory ought to provide a link with aggregative economics, then the theory ought to be extended to incorporate at least production, money, time, and expectations.

The theory, as it will be developed here, will not appear to have much flesh on it. It will not have much to say about how a poor man can survive in a rich country; it will not be able to answer a critic of a capitalist society's spending on military projects. Rather the theory will provide the bare outlines of an ascetic's view of the economic process. Like all abstractions, the model possesses a formal beauty in the elegance of its argument. But this is of secondary importance.

What is worth emphasising is that any argument about economics depends on a logic, or the process that enables one to draw conclusions from certain premises. If the economist is to be more than an observer or a data-collector he must explain economic phenomena. To do this requires models, simplified of necessity, of the processes he wishes to study.

General equilibrium theory is the most complete existing model of economic behaviour. If it is too simple at present, complexity must be introduced; if it is too rigid, flexibility must be incorporated; if it leads to erroneous conclusions, the assumptions must be modified in order that the model may be of some use in organising diverse events.

Barring logical error, a model is neither correct nor incorrect, neither true nor false. It is only more or less useful for the purposes at hand. Thus a model may be modified as economists ask more sophisticated questions, or even different questions. At worst, a model may be misleading if it directs attention to peripheral issues; at best it may be a superb tool if it leads economists to ask new and interesting questions. It is in this spirit that the models of the following chapters will be presented.

2 An Exchange Model

FROM THE SPECIFIC TO THE GENERAL

Very often treatments of the general equilibrium problem begin with the abstract formulation, leaving to the reader's intuition the concrete realisation of the elegant mathematical propositions. But another course is possible. It should be clear that any discussion of general equilibrium theory based on general optimising behaviour of individual units must be reconcilable with particular forms of such behaviour. The discussion which follows will thus use a concrete (specific functional form) representation of individual behaviour; in this way the economic content of the discussion will not become lost in a welter of formal theorems. It is then a simple matter to extract general ideas from the particular form in which those ideas have been embodied.

The model to be considered represents the rudimentary and unrealistic case of a barter society. In a pure trade context, individuals exchange fixed stocks of goods. Imagine, for instance, hunters, fishermen, and farmers coming to market to exchange their goods, where each desires a balanced diet requiring meat, fish, and grain. Goods are thus in perfectly inelastic supply, so a study of the markets for commodities depends only on the demand for those commodities.

THE MODEL

If x_i represents amounts of the ith good, and the vector $x = (x_1, \ldots x_n)$ is the vector of amounts of all goods, suppose that x_i^j represents the amount of good i that trader j would like.

Since the jth trader may be thought of as an agent who can rank various outcomes, in each of which he receives a different basket of goods, trader j has a preference among bundles of the form $x^j = (x_1^j, x_2^j, \ldots x_n^j)$. If he is rational [11], and if his preferences satisfy some other properties [12], then it is possible to attach a number to each of those outcomes such that 'more preferred' outcomes have 'larger numbers'. The rule, or function, which assigns numbers to outcomes in this manner is the utility function.

Let the utility function for trader j be given by U^j. This depends on x^j; assume that the function is given in a specific form by

$$U^j(x^j) = \sum_{k=1}^{n} a_k^j \log x_k^j \qquad (2.1)$$

where a_k is a constant with $0 < a_k < 1$, and $\sum_{k=1}^{n} a_k = 1$.

Intuitively, the utility level depends on the amounts trader j has of goods $x_1^j, \ldots x_n^j$; if x_1^j, say, increases, then trader j's utility goes up by the natural logarithm of x_1^j. The a_k^j weight the contribution of the good to utility. If a_1^j were large, and a_2^j were small, then good one would be more important to trader j's utility level than good two.

The budget constraint, or income, of trader j certainly depends on the goods he can sell; thus let $\bar{x}_i^j$ be the stock of good i that trader j brings to market. If perfect competition prevails, so that the price, p_i, of the ith good is given to trader j, his income is $p_1\bar{x}_1^j + p_2\bar{x}_2^j + \ldots p_n\bar{x}_n^j$, which will be denoted by I^j.

The optimisation problem faced by the jth trader is thus clear: maximise $\sum_{k}^{n} a_k^j \log x_k^j$ subject to $p_1x_1^j + \ldots p_nx_n^j = I^j$. That is, for given a_k^j and p_k, what vector of goods $(x_1^j, \ldots x_n^j)$ will yield the greatest utility assuming that that bundle can be purchased out of trader j's income?

Using Lagrange multiplier techniques for solving such constrained optimisation problems yields the result that the quantity demanded of good i by trader j depends on *his* income and all prices. For the above problem, one finds that the demand function is given by

$$D_i^j(p_1, \ldots p_n; I^j) = a_i^j I^j / p_i. \qquad (2.2)$$

So far, then, from assumptions of fixed stocks of goods, perfect competition, the existence of utility functions, and utility maximisation subject to budget constraints, individual demand functions have been derived for each trader. How is it

20

possible now to develop the general equilibrium schema, involving market excess demand expressions?

EXCESS DEMAND

If there are n traders, one way of proceeding is by aggregation. That is, if the total or aggregate or market demand for good i is the sum of all the individual demands for good i, one gets

$$D_i(p_1, \ldots p_n; I) = \sum_{j=1}^{m} D_i^j(p_1, \ldots p_n; I^j) \qquad (2.3)$$

or, for the specific model used,

$$D_i(p_1, \ldots p_n; I) = \sum_{j=1}^{m} a_i^j I^j / p_i, \qquad (2.4)$$

where $I = I^1 + I^2 + \ldots I^m$

As in all aggregation problems, it is necessary to make strong simplifying assumptions about the individual units otherwise the units cannot be added. Thus assume that all individuals have similar tastes, so that $a_i^j = a_i^k \equiv a_i$ for any traders j and k. The market demand curves become

$$D_i(p_1, \ldots p_n; I) = \frac{a_i}{p_i} \sum_{j=1}^{m} I^i. \qquad (2.5)$$

Now clearly the total stock, in society, of good i is the sum of the stocks of good i held by all m traders: denoting the total stock by $\bar{x}_i$, one has

$$\bar{x}_i = \sum_{j=1}^{m} \bar{x}_i^j.$$

Since

$$I^j = \sum_{i=1}^{n} p_i \bar{x}_i^j \qquad (2.6)$$

and

$$I = \sum_{j=1}^{m} I^j,$$

(2.5) may be written as

21

$$D_i(p_1, \ldots p_n; I) = \frac{a_i}{p_i} I, \qquad (2.7)$$

so that the market demand function is

$$D_i(p_1, \ldots p_n; I) = \frac{a_i}{p_i} \left(\sum_{i=1}^{n} p_i \bar{x}_i \right). \qquad (2.8)$$

Clearly the ith market supply function is just $\bar{x}_i$. Hence the market excess demand function for good i is (suppressing I)

$$E_i(p_1, \ldots p_n) = \frac{a_i}{p_i} (p_1 \bar{x}_1 + \ldots p_n \bar{x}_n) - \bar{x}_i, \qquad (2.9)$$

or

$$E_i(p_1, \ldots p_n) = \frac{a_i}{p_i} [p_1 \bar{x}_1 + \ldots \left(1 - \frac{1}{a_i} \right) p_i \bar{x}_i + \ldots p_n \bar{x}_n]. \ (2.10)$$

The general equilibrium model of an exchange economy, under the assumptions developed above, can thus be written down completely as

$$E_1(p_1, \ldots p_n) = \frac{a_1}{p_1} \left[\left(1 - \frac{1}{a_1} \right) p_1 \bar{x}_1 + p_2 \bar{x}_2 + \ldots p_n \bar{x}_n \right]$$

$$E_2(p_1, \ldots p_n) = \frac{a_2}{p_2} [p_1 \bar{x}_1 + \left(1 - \frac{1}{a_2} \right) p_2 \bar{x}_2 + \ldots p_n \bar{x}_n]$$

$$\vdots$$

$$E_n(p_1, \ldots p_n) = \frac{a_n}{p_n} [p_1 \bar{x}_1 + p_2 \bar{x}_2 + \ldots \left(1 - \frac{1}{a_n} \right) p_n \bar{x}_n]. \qquad (2.11)$$

EQUILIBRIUM

Under what conditions will there exist a positive price vector $p = (p_1^e, p_2^e, \ldots p_n^e)$ (i.e., $p_i^e > 0$ for some i and $p_j^e \geqslant 0$ for all j) such that $E_i(p_1^e, p_2^e, \ldots p_n^e) = 0$ for all goods i? That is, what circumstances or conditions on 2.11 will ensure that an equilibrium set of prices exists?

In the case of the system 2.11 the answer is clear:

Proposition 2.1: There exists a positive equilibrium price vector for the general equilibrium system 2.11.

Proof: By inspection, $p_i^e = a_i/\bar{x}_i$, $i = 1,2, \ldots n$, is a solution to equation 2.11. (To check this, the reader should substitute, say, $p_1 = a_1/\bar{x}_1$ into E_1 above.) Clearly $p_i^e > 0$ for all i, since for all i, $a_i > 0$, and $\bar{x}_i$ is finite. Q.e.d.

Is this equilibrium unique? Consider

$$\frac{a_1}{p_1}\left[\left(1-\frac{1}{a_1}\right)p_1\bar{x}_1+p_2\bar{x}_2+\ldots p_n\bar{x}_n\right]=0$$

$$\frac{a_2}{p_2}\left[p_1\bar{x}_1+\left(1-\frac{1}{a_2}\right)p_2\bar{x}_2+\ldots p_n\bar{x}_n\right]=0$$

$$\vdots$$

$$\frac{a_n}{p_n}\left[p_1\bar{x}_1+p_2\bar{x}_2+\ldots\left(1-\frac{1}{a_n}\right)p_n\bar{x}_n\right]=0 \qquad (2.12)$$

This is a system of n homogeneous linear equations in the n unknowns $p_1,\ldots p_n$ which had $p_i=a_i/\bar{x}_i$ as one solution. It is known from the theory of equations, though, that any non-trivial solution is not unique [13].

WALRAS' LAW

Alternatively, multiply the first equation of 2.11 by p_1, the second by p_2, etc., and add all the resulting equations. One finds that the sum of the left sides is zero, no matter what the values of $p_1,\ldots p_n$ might be. That is,

$$p_1E_1(p_1,\ldots p_n;I)+p_2E_2(p_1,\ldots p_n;I)+\ldots$$
$$p_nE_n(p_1,\ldots p_n;I)\equiv 0, \qquad (2.13)$$

since

$$p_1\frac{a_1}{p_1}\left[\left(1-\frac{1}{a_1}\right)p_1\bar{x}_1+\ldots p_n\bar{x}_n\right]+\ldots p_n\frac{a_n}{p_n}\left[p_1\bar{x}_1+\ldots\right.$$
$$\left.\left(1-\frac{1}{a_1}\right)p_n\bar{x}_n\right]=0. \text{ (The reader should check this.)}$$

Thus

$$\sum_{j=1}^{n}p_iE_i(p_1,\ldots p_n;I)\equiv 0. \qquad (2.14)$$

In other words, there is a linear dependence among the n equations of the system 2.11, so one equation of that system is redundant. Essentially, there are $n-1$ independent equations in the n unknowns $p_1,\ldots p_n$ [14].

If the price of one good is fixed, say $p_n=\bar{p}_n$, then $(p_1/\bar{p}_n,\ldots p_{n-1}/\bar{p}_n,1)$ are $n-1$ relative prices, which can be determined from any $n-1$ of the equations in 2.11. The nth good in this case is termed the 'numeraire', and all other goods are expressed in terms of its price [14]. (One may think of good n as the unit of account.)

Relationship 2.14 has some interesting interpretations. It is

23

termed *Walras' Law*; breaking E_i, the excess demand function, into its component demand and supply functions, it states that the *value* of demand is identically equal to the *value* of supply, or expenditures equal receipts. It is an intriguing corollary to Walras' Law that if the first $n-1$ markets in a system are in equilibrium, then the nth is as well. (To see this, write 2.14 as $\sum_{i=1}^{n-1} p_i E_i = -p_n E_n$. If the first $n-1$ markets are in equilibrium, then $E_i = 0$ for $i = 1,2, \ldots n-1$. Thus $-p_n E_n = 0$. But since $p_n \neq 0$, $E_n = 0$ so the nth market is in equilibrium.)

One related property of the system of excess demand equations (2.11) is that they are *homogeneous of degree zero in prices*. That is, if prices double, or triple, or are cut in half, then excess demand is unchanged. To see this, consider the ith equation in 2.11,

$$E_i(p_1, \ldots p_n) = \frac{a_i}{p_i} [p_1 \bar{x}_1 + \ldots \left(1 - \frac{1}{a_i}\right) p_i \bar{x}_i + \ldots p_n \bar{x}_n]. \quad (2.15)$$

If $p_1^* = 2p_1$, $p_2^* = 2p_2$, $\ldots p_n^* = 2p_n$, so that prices moving from p to p^* means prices have doubled,

$$E_i(p_1^*, p_2^*, \ldots p_n^*) = \frac{a_i}{p_i^*} [p_1^* \bar{x}_1 + \ldots \left(1 - \frac{1}{a_i}\right)$$

$$p_i^* \bar{x}_i + \ldots p_n^* \bar{x}_n]$$

$$= \frac{a_i}{2p_i} [2p_1 \bar{x}_1 + \ldots \left(1 - \frac{1}{a_i}\right) 2p_i \bar{x}_i + \ldots 2p_n \bar{x}_n]$$

$$= \frac{2a_i}{2p_i} [p_1 x_1 + \ldots \left(1 - \frac{1}{a_i}\right) p_i \bar{x}_i + \ldots p_n \bar{x}_n]$$

$$= E_i[p_1, \ldots p_n].$$

It is the homogeneity of the excess demands which really gives the relative price solution to the system its character. For if the equilibrium was $p_i = a_i/\bar{x}_i$ for all i, then $p_i = 2a_i/\bar{x}_i$ would also be an equilibrium, as would $p_i = 7a_i/8\bar{x}_i$.

Thus the equilibrium price vector is not unique; it is however unique up to multiplication by a constant so it follows that *the equilibrium set of $n-1$ relative prices is unique*.

In summary, the general equilibrium system was characterised by (a) the utility function $U_j(X) = \sum_{k=1}^{n} a_k^j \log \bar{x}_k^j$; (b) similar individuals; (c) utility maximisation under the budget constraint; (d) perfect competition; (e) fixed stocks of goods; and (f) equilibrium defined to be the price vector equating supply and demand. For this general equilibrium system, a unique equilibrium set of relative prices was shown to exist.

What, if anything, can be learned from this specific example about the existence of equilibrium for a general system? Actually, there is a good deal, since all salient aspects of the general case are contained in the specific example. If instead of the specific utility function and identical individuals (assumptions (a) and (b) above) the only requirement is that the utility function for each individual satisfy certain general properties, it remains true that an equilibrium set of relative prices exists.

In particular, let it be assumed that (1) all individual utility functions are differentiable; (2) for any indifference curve associated with any individual utility function, there is always a higher indifference level (non-satiation); and (3) the set of points lying on and above any indifference curve (which is linked to any trader's utility function) is strictly convex.[1] Then *an exchange* economy characterised by assumptions (c), (d), (e), (f), (1), (2) and (3) has an equilibrium vector of relative prices [15].

STABILITY

Given that an equilibrium price set *exists* for the specific model, the standard question arises: does the system ever attain the equilibrium? Any discussion of the properties of that equilibrium, like its optimality in a sense to be defined later, must be misleading if it cannot be established that the system actually reaches the equilibrium position.

As the discussion of Chapter 1 indicated, it is impossible to discuss these matters without specifying the dynamic rules of the model, the rules which say how arbitrary states (price vectors) are transformed into new states (new prices). How do

[1] A *set* is *convex* if a line segment, joining any two points in the set, lies wholly within the set.

The reader may wish to construct the two-dimensional indifference curves of $U_j(x_1,x_2) = a_1^j x_1 + a_2^j x_2$, $a_1^j + a_2^j = 1$, $a_1^j, a_2^j > 0$, to verify non-satiation and strict convexity in the example.

prices change, or more specifically, how does the price of the ith good, p_i, change?

Standard practice in this matter is to assume the presence of the Walrasian tatonnement, the dynamic adjustment mechanism given by the rule: if the excess demand for any commodity is positive, its price rises, and if excess demand is negative, price falls, and no trades are consummated until equilibrium is attained.

In contradistinction to a single market model, here excess demand for one good depends on *all* prices, so the movements of all prices are interrelated. Can anything be said in general about stability?

Consider a market of n goods in which three goods, A, B, and C, are all substitutes for one another. So, for example, if P_A increases, excess demand for B and C increases. Suppose the B and C markets are in equilibrium, with zero excess demand (which depends among other prices on the prices P_A, P_B, P_C). Now suppose there is positive excess demand for A; A's price rises towards equilibrium. As A's price increases, excess demand for B and C increases, thus increasing P_B and P_C. Consequently excess demand for A falls, so P_A falls, so excess demand for B and C decreases, dropping their prices. If all the goods are substitutes, then, it seems as though wild changes in prices are somewhat damped by the Walrasian mechanism.

Suppose, however, that the three goods are complements, so an increase in P_A will lead to a decrease in excess demand for B and C. Again suppose the B and C markets are in equilibrium, and there is excess demand for good A. As P_A increases to equilibrium, excess demand for B and C falls, lowering P_B and P_C. But this means that excess demand for A increases, increasing P_A still further, and so on. Complements thus appear to promote unstable price behaviour.

Is the system defined by equations 2.11 characterised by substitutability or complementarity? As, say, p_j increases, does E_i increase or decrease? To answer this question it clearly suffices to compute $\delta E_i(p_1, \ldots p_n; I)/\delta p_j$ for $i \neq j$.[1] If this is positive, goods i and j are gross substitutes, if negative, gross complements. But

[1] As a technical point, *substitutability* usually refers to compensated price changes; the case here is one of *gross substitutability*.

$$\frac{\delta E_i}{\delta p_j} = \frac{\delta}{\delta p_j}\left[\frac{a_i}{p_i}\left\{p_1\bar{x}_1 + \ldots \left(1-\frac{1}{a_i}\right)p_i\bar{x}_i + \ldots p_n\bar{x}_n\right\}\right]$$

$$= \frac{\delta}{\delta p_j}\left(\frac{a_i}{p_i}p_j x_j\right) = \frac{a_i}{p_j}x_j > 0.$$

In other words, all goods in the particular system are strong gross substitutes for one another. (Strong refers to $(\delta E_i/\delta p_j) > 0$, weak entails $(\delta E_i/\delta p_j) \gtreqqless 0$.)

In the single market, the normalcy of the demand curve, its negative slope, entailed stability. Clearly it is a stabilising fact that an increase in the price of any good, other prices constant, leads to a fall in the demand (and excess demand) for that good. One is thus led to inquire about the negativity of $\delta E_i/\delta p_i$.

Differentiation yields

$$\frac{\delta E_i}{\delta p_i} = \frac{\delta}{\delta p_i}\left[\frac{a_i}{p_i}\left\{p_1\bar{x}_1 + \ldots \left(1-\frac{1}{a_i}\right)p_i\bar{x}_i + \ldots p_n\bar{x}_n\right\}\right]$$

$$= \frac{a_i}{p_i}\left(1-\frac{1}{a_i}\right)\bar{x}_i + [p_1\bar{x}_1 + \ldots \left(1-\frac{1}{a_i}\right)p_i\bar{x}_i + \ldots p_n\bar{x}_n]\frac{-a_i}{p_i^2}$$

$$= \frac{a_i}{p_i^2}\left[\left(1-\frac{1}{a_i}\right)p_i\bar{x}_i - \left\{p_1\bar{x}_1 + \ldots \left(1-\frac{1}{a_i}\right)p_i\bar{x}_i + \ldots p_n\bar{x}_n\right\}\right]$$

$$= \frac{a_i}{p_i^2}\left[-p_1\bar{x}_1 - p_2\bar{x}_2 - \ldots p_{i-1}\bar{x}_{i-1} - 0 - p_{i+1}\bar{x}_{i+1}\right.$$

$$\left. - \ldots p_n\bar{x}_n\right] < 0.$$

Consequently, the own price effect on excess demand $(\delta E_i/\delta p_i)$ is negative, and the cross price effects $(\delta E_i/\delta p_j)$ are positive.

While both these conditions suggest that stability will be present they do not constitute a proof. Since the mathematics of such a demonstration would require considerable sophistication, the following general theorem, presented here without proof, must suffice: *An exchange economy, with a Walrasian price adjustment mechanism, will possess a stable equilibrium provided (a) the excess demand functions are homogeneous of degree zero in prices, (b) Walras' Law obtains and (c) strong gross substitutability is present* [15].

A purely heuristic argument may help to justify this assertion. In some sense, if the negativity of the own price effect outweighs the positivity of all the cross effects in every excess demand function, then any such function will be similar to the negatively sloped excess demand function in the stable single market case. Homogeneity and Walras' Law, as regularity conditions on the set of excess demand functions, serve to relate the various own and cross price effects in such a way that, when gross substitutability prevails, the own effects dominate.

There are two points worth noting here. On the one hand the theorem only provides a set of sufficient conditions for stability – it may be that systems not characterised by such assumptions are stable. Thus the existence of complementarities in the 'real world' does not imply that the theorem is useless, since stronger theorems may someday be proved.

On the other hand, it is possible to argue that something very much like the gross substitutability assumption is likely to be necessary. If so, it can be supposed that stability is a rather unlikely state of affairs, at least in this simple model world. It might be, as a result of this, that various institutions and arrangements in the real world, which intuitively seems stable, arise from the 'natural' tendency of the system to exhibit unstable price movements [16]. The existence of long-term contractual agreements in money terms, for instance, tend to inhibit excessive price movements to the degree that such movements arise from uncertain price expectations [17].

3 The Trading Game

There is another way, complementary to that of Chapter 2, of examining general equilibrium models of exchange. Instead of specifying a general model to analyse an exchange economy, it is possible to explore partial exchange situations alone, then build up to a general model. In this chapter the mechanics and logic of simple two-person exchanges will be extended to multi-person, multi-good exchanges thus leading to a general equilibrium system. As the focus is on exchange, the theorems will have a somewhat different flavour from those of the previous chapter; they will however illuminate certain facets of the Walrasian model [18, 11].

The starting point for the analysis is the preference structure of the individual trader. As before, non-satiation, strict convexity, and continuity of preferences are assumed. Further, let it be hypothesised that the traders have at least some goods. From these facts, it can be shown that the set of goods baskets at least as preferred as the initial basket (x_0), called the 'better set for x_0' and denoted $B(x_0)$, is a convex set (see Fig. 3) [11].

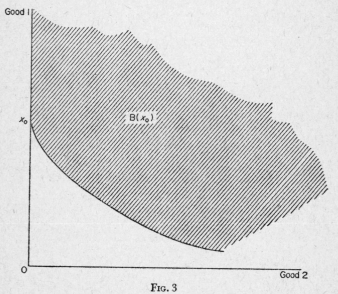

Fig. 3

29

Fig. 3 has been drawn showing an initial basket containing only good 1.

For two traders, the geometric device of the Edgeworth Box diagram can be used to illustrate the initial holdings and better sets of each.

In Fig. 4 the situation represented in Fig. 3, for each trader, has been combined by reflecting the axis for individual B and superimposing B's 'picture' on that for A. The vertical axis represents the total amount of good 1 available for trade, the horizontal that of good 2. Point x_0 is the vector (pair) of initial holdings, and indifference curves through x_0, one each for A and B, show goods baskets towards which the traders are indifferent. For example, the point x' represents x_1 of good 1 and x_2 of good 2, and trader A is indifferent between baskets x_0 and x'.

If traders will only exchange goods when they are not made worse off by so doing, it is obvious that the set of baskets for which trade is *feasible* is represented by the intersection of the two better sets, $B(x_0)$, for each individual (see Fig. 5).

Any basket in the interior of that region (off both indifference curves) makes both traders better off than their initial holdings represented by x_0. For example, in Fig. 6, the point x assigns bundles (x_1^A, x_2^A) to A, and (x_1^B, x_2^B) to B, and lies on indifference curve I^A for A, and I^B for B.

But I^A is a higher indifference curve for A than that which passes through x_0, so A prefers x to x_0; similarly for B. Basket x is thus a feasible trade and it is attainable as well since it merely requires trader A to offer x_1^B of his holdings of good 1 to B in exchange for x_2^A of B's holdings of good 2. No resources are sacrificed in making the trade.

Suppose that the traders have x_0, and that A suggests the allocation (the trade implicit in the allocation) x in Fig. 6. Could any other trades be made which would be preferred, by both parties, to x? Clearly trade x^* would be better than x, since it would lie on a higher indifference curve for each. Thus if A suggested x, B could countersuggest x^*, and since x^* is feasible, and attainable, and since it *dominates* x (is at least as preferred by all parties and is strictly preferred by at least one individual), x would not be chosen. Are there any feasible, attainable allocations that dominate x^*? From Fig. 7 it is clear that any x^{***} which lies on a point of tangency between A's indifference curves and B's indifference curves in the feasible

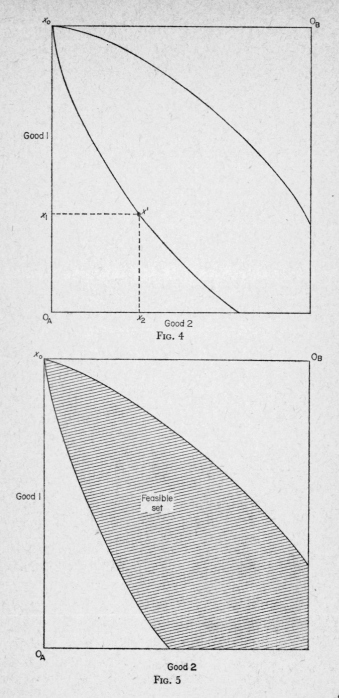

FIG. 4

FIG. 5

31

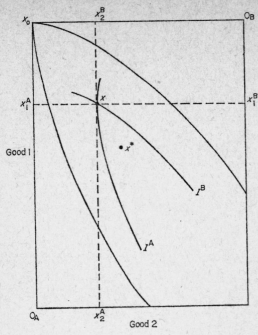

Fig. 6

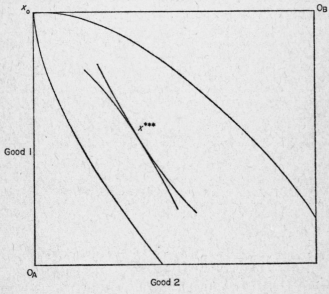

Fig. 7

trading region is (a) attainable[1] from x_0, and (b) feasible. Further, any point that is not a point of tangency is dominated by a tangency point.

By definition, the contract curve (trading curve, or conflict curve) is the set of points of tangency between the two indifference curve systems (see Fig. 8) through points in the feasible region.

It is obvious that points on the contract curve are undominated. From game theory, a set of feasible, attainable,

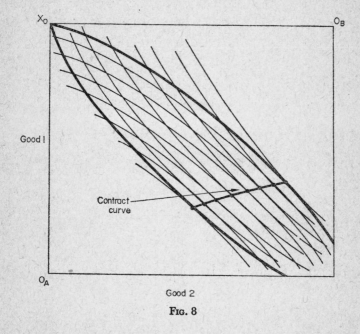

FIG. 8

and undominated allocations is called the *core* of the game. Since trading is a game in the formal sense, with payoffs, preferences over outcomes, etc., the core of the trading game *is* the contract curve [19, 20].

Another important definition may now be introduced. An allocation (of goods or traders or market participants) is *Pareto-optimal* if any other allocation makes at least one trader strictly worse off. Consider any point on the contract curve. A movement to any point *off* the contract curve moves either

---

[1] Every allocation in the Edgeworth Box is 'attainable'; i.e. any such basket can be achieved by some trade.

A or B to a strictly lower indifference curve. Similarly a movement from one point on the contract curve to another point on the curve makes one trader worse off. Thus the set of Pareto-optimal allocations, in this two-person, two-good exchange model with initial distribution x_0, *is* the contract curve, *is* the core.

It is from the concepts of the core and Pareto-optimality that the equilibrium notion for the two-person trading model is obtained. Recall that, in general, a state is an equilibrium one if, when the system is in that state, there is no tendency for the system to leave that state, where 'tendency' pertains to the rules or dynamics which govern change in the system. The rules of the trading game suggest that traders will never exchange at *dominated* allocations. Only undominated, or core, allocations are viable. Thus if states of the system are all allocations in the Edgeworth Box, and all such states are attainable, the rules exclude firstly infeasible trades outside the intersection of the better sets. Further, the rules preclude outcomes, or states, off the contract curve since the traders can attain the allocations on the contract curve, and are better off on the curve than off it. The core thus does represent the equilibrium for the model.

With the assumptions made about preferences, it is known that there *is* a contract curve, as the figures drawn show [11]. For this trading model, then, an equilibrium exists; the core, as a set, is non-empty. Unfortunately, though, as the geometry suggests, the equilibrium is not unique, since *any* point on the contract curve is an equilibrium point.

UNIQUENESS OF THE EQUILIBRIUM

The rules of making offers or counter-offers, and thus of reaching a core allocation, do not determine *which* core allocation is attained. Some indeterminacy is present: without an external mechanism to fix *the* equilibrium, the solution is incomplete. It may be argued, for instance, that points on the contract curve near A's original indifference curve represent little gain from trade for A, and a large gain for B. Thus bargaining strength might settle the ultimate outcome. For this reason, the contract curve is called, by some, the *conflict curve*. Forgoing this approach, though, there still remain natural mechanisms to determine the outcome.

The differences between the two-person exchange model and the Walrasian exchange system suggest a resolution of the problem. For two major issues have not been broached: first, what is the role of prices, and second, what is the effect of introducing m traders in n commodities? This subsection will look at the price system, while the next examines more goods and traders.

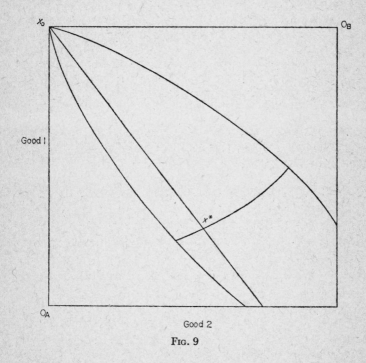

FIG. 9

Suppose, then, that the two-person, two-good model is embedded in a perfectly competitive price system, so that whatever the prices of the two goods, they are exogenous to decisions made by the traders to offer exchanges. In Fig. 9 any pair of prices for goods 1 and 2 will determine their relative prices. Since the traders have the option of not trading whatever the prices, a straight line through x_0 reflects a price ratio. For example, in Fig. 9, if the unit price of 1 is p_1 and of 2 p_2, p_2/p_1 is the slope of the price line passing through x_0. Any allocation along that line reflects the fact that p_1 units of good 1 are equivalent to p_2 units of good 2. If p_1 and p_2 are given, so

35

the price system is given to the traders, what allocation will be attained? The answer is clear: the equilibrium allocation, which must lie on the contract curve, is represented by the intersection of the price line with the core. The equilibrium is x^*.

Intuitively, a solution reflecting little gain for A is reached by a steeply sloped line, where p_2/p_1 is large. Thus a unit of good 2 is worth a great deal of good 1. The individual initially holding good 2, trader B, is thus able to extract a large gain from trade with A.

A competitive equilibrium is an allocation of goods to traders such that, for a competitive price system, the allocation is the best that the traders can achieve. Thus the immediate result is that every competitive equilibrium, in the two-person trading model, is in the core. Further, every competitive equilibrium is Pareto-optimal; any non-competitive equilibrium involves a worse-off position for at least one trader. These results will be reconsidered later in this chapter.

MANY TRADERS AND MANY GOODS

It should be geometrically obvious that the introduction of more goods does not alter the analysis. For three goods, for instance, the indifference 'curves' are surfaces in a three-dimensional space, each axis representing amounts of the good. The Edgeworth Box is a rectangular solid, the feasible set is still convex, the contract curve or core is still a curve (because the better sets are strictly convex), and the price line is a plane whose direction is determined by the two price ratios and x_0. The intersection of the core with the price plane is a point, a unique triple of goods which determines the allocations to each trader. Passing from three goods to n goods makes no further difference [11].

But suppose that there are two traders exactly like A, and two exactly like B, for two goods. Do the results obtained above still hold?

It is easy to see that there are some new complications, since there are now more exchange possibilities. Each A-type trader can trade with each B-type trader, or both, and conversely. Let the four traders be denoted $A_\alpha, A_\beta, B_\alpha, B_\beta$. Suppose that the allocation at the end of the original contract curve for A and B, nearest O_A, was suggested. (Here A_α and A_β each have half of A's initial holdings, likewise for the B-types [11].) Fig. 10 shows this pictorially.

Consider the box with the indifference maps for each trader of each type superimposed on one another, so x_0 represents the total initial holdings, and I_A is the initial indifference curve for

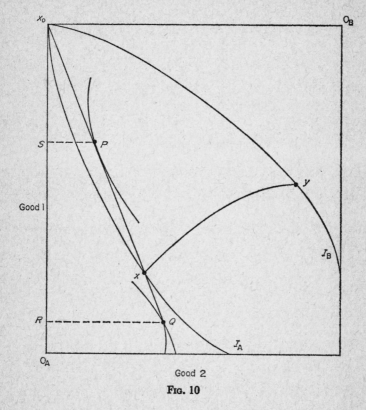

FIG. 10

traders A_α and A_β. Suppose x is suggested. Now pick some point Q, below x, which lies on the line x_0x. Choose P to be half of x_0Q. Drop perpendiculars from P and Q to the line 0_Ax_0 to locate S and R. Thus x_0S is half x_0R, and SP is half RQ. Let trader B_α offer the following exchange: B_α will give up RQ of good 2 in exchange for x_0R of good 1 where x_0S is supplied by each of A_α and A_β.

Both A_α and A_β thus supply x_0S and receive SP. But since P lies on a higher indifference curve than x, each A trader is better off under this allocation. Trader B_α supplies RQ of good

37

2 to get x_0R of good 1, so B_α ends up at point Q which is on a higher indifference curve (for the B's) than is x, so B_α is better off.

Hence the point x on the original contract curve is dominated; it cannot be in the core!

Of course trader B_β will not stand idly outside the trading process. With B_β making counter-offers to A_α and A_β, it is clear that the only undominated allocations must continue to lie on the contract curve. Since a reversal of A's and B's above shows that y is not a core allocation, the result appears that the core, or equilibrium, for this four-person, two-good trading model is a *proper subset* of the core for the two-person, two-good model.

In short, the contract curve, and the set of Pareto-optimal allocations, is not changed by the introduction of more traders, but the core shrinks.

It should be apparent that a further increase in the number of traders of each type will lead to a still smaller core; incorporating the facts about n goods shows that *the core of an* n-*good* m-*trader exchange model is a proper subset of the core of an* n-*good,* (m − 1)-*trader exchange model.* Further, every core allocation is a Pareto-optimal allocation; this fact can be seen intuitively as well since allowing *only* coalitions of traders which include *all* traders prevents the shrinkage argument from working, so in that case viable (core) allocations must make no trader worse off, so every Pareto-optimal allocation is in the core.

THE LIMIT THEOREM

The importance of these results should not be lost through understatement, since they are among the deepest and most intellectually satisfying in all of economic theory. If the only reason for introducing the price system, and perfect competition modelled by exogeneous prices, was to select a particular allocation in the core as *the* equilibrium, then clearly the price system is redundant in a world of many traders. Since adding traders reduces the size of the core, the natural idea is that with 'very' many traders, the core will shrink to a point, and that allocation will be the equilibrium. These rough ideas have been given form and established by Shubik [20], Debreu and Scarf [21], and Aumann [22] following the brilliant lead given almost a century ago by Edgeworth. In particular, it has been proved that as the number of traders of each type increases without limit, the core shrinks *towards* a single allocation. This theorem, called the *Limit Theorem*, has been given its ultimate form by Aumann, who proved that if the traders were represented by points in the interval (0, 1), so that there were an uncountably infinite number of traders of *n* commodities, then the core is a *single* allocation, the competitive equilibrium. Since a line (or plane) can be drawn through the core and the initial allocation, a price system in relative prices is determined, and the core is the competitive equilibrium with respect to that system.

It is the presence of many traders which determines the equilibrium for the trading system, and not an externally imposed price system. The most important ramification of this result is that if perfect competition is conceived to be modelled by very many completely ineffectual (individual) traders, then it is perfect competition which entails the existence of a general equilibrium set of (relative) prices.

In contradistinction to the Walrasian view in which the markets and market relationships determine the equilibrium of the system, the Edgeworthian view has competition for goods, independent of prices, as the property which realises the system's equilibrium.

DYNAMICS

Granted that an equilibrium exists for a multi-person, multi-good exchange system, what are the rules which determine how states (allocations) change over time? A counterpart of the Walrasian tatonnement is required to move the initial allocation to other allocations, to the equilibrium if the process is in fact stable.

The device created by Edgeworth was 're-contracting'. That is, suppose an allocation different from the initial allocation is suggested by some coalition of traders [23]. If the suggested allocation is feasible, and attainable, and dominates the initial allocation, let the traders contract to exchange at this allocation. If this new allocation is in the core, it is not dominated by any other allocation and it is an equilibrium. If it is not in the core, then it is dominated by some other feasible, attainable exchange. If knowledge is perfect, some coalition of traders can thus suggest another allocation which dominates the trade already contracted for. If traders are permitted to re-contract, they will, since they are better off.

It is not difficult to see that this process will terminate only when a suggested allocation is undominated, or in the core. Since the core is the equilibrium for the system, the device of recontracting and of coalition formation is a dynamic process which leads to equilibrium outcomes. If there were a cost (in terms of goods) to re-contract, or an information cost to form coalitions, the original equilibrium would not necessarily be attained. Further, if traders actually effected exchanges at dominated allocations, there is no guarantee that such a disequilibrium trading process would lead to the competitive allocation [24, 25].

WELFARE IMPLICATIONS

Since this work is concerned with general equilibrium analysis rather than welfare economics, only a few remarks need to be made about the welfare, or social choice, implications of the preceding sections.

In assessing two different positions for society, where 'positions' are allocations of goods and 'society' is modelled by the exchange system, it is usually impossible to make comparisons of well-being, or preference, since often some individuals are made worse off by the movement, and others are made better off. Without some criterion for weighting gains and losses, the usual sorts of optimality arguments founder. If, however, it can be determined that a movement from allocation x to allocation x^* makes no individual worse off, and at least one better off, then x^* is said to be better. Thus Pareto-optimal allocations are 'best' in the sense that any other allocation makes at least one individual worse off.

A defence of perfect competition is often based on the Pareto-optimality of the equilibrium or core allocations discussed above. This point shall be reconsidered when production, money, and expectations are introduced into the system.

4 Expectations and Production

Models of exchange, like those presented in previous chapters, provide only a first approximation to the kind of system that economists require to generate realistic aggregative structures. Keynes, for example, argued that the *General Theory* must include short- and long-term expectations, production, and money [26], and that a theory which placed these elements in a minor or supporting role had little explanatory power.

In this chapter both expectations and production will be introduced to extend the standard exchange model. The system which results will thus begin to resemble a stylised market economy, though not until the role of money is brought into focus can there be hope that the likeness will be more than a superficial one.

PRICE EXPECTATIONS

Consider the demand functions, embedded in the excess demand functions, of the exchange system. For each good the quantity demanded of that good depends on the price of that and all other commodities. The precise form of the dependence emerges from the given preferences of the individual traders and the value of the stocks which form their budget constraints.

If, however, one extends the time horizon by one period, then desired purchases today depend not only on today's complete configuration of prices but also on tomorrow's. If the demand for television sets depends on all prices today, and a trader expects the price of television sets tomorrow to fall, then he might defer his purchases for one period. Similarly, if the price of radio sets were expected to be lower in the future, this expectation, if held with confidence, might influence the decision to purchase a television today.

If the prices of the n goods in the system are as usual denoted $p_1, \ldots p_n$, let $p_1^*, \ldots p_n^*$ denote currently held expectations of future prices, where the future represents the next trading period. (If there are m traders in the model world, it might seem that, if each trader holds different views of the future, one would need to define $p_{11}^*, p_{21}^*, \ldots p_{n1}^*, \ldots p_{1m}^*, p_{2m}^*, \ldots p_{nm}^*$. It can be shown, however, that if traders hold differing expectations of future prices no analytic difficulties beyond notational inconvenience are introduced [27]. For this reason it will be assumed that all traders have identical price expectations.)

The effect of introducing price expectations may be seen first in the excess demand equations of the exchange system. If x_i is the quantity demanded of commodity i, and $\bar{x}_i$ is the total stock of that good, then excess demand for good i is $x_i - \bar{x}_i$; but whereas previously x_i depended on current prices as $x_i = D_i(p_1, \ldots p_n)$, now it depends on current prices *and* currently held expectations of future prices, as $x_i = D_i(p_1, \ldots p_n; p_1^*, \ldots p_n^*)$.[1]

EQUILIBRIUM

As noted in Chapter 1, an equilibrium state of any system is a state such that, if the system is in that state, there is no tendency for the system to move from that state. But what constitutes a state of the general equilibrium system when expectations are present?

If the system is taken to be the complete set of excess demand equations, $D_i - \bar{x}_i = E_i$, together with the tatonnement rule that current prices move in the direction of excess demand, then the system would look like

$$E_1 = D_1(p_1, \ldots p_n; p_1^*, \ldots p_n^*) - \bar{x}_1$$
$$E_2 = D_2(p_1, \ldots p_n; p_1^*, \ldots p_n^*) - \bar{x}_2$$
$$\vdots$$
$$E_n = D_n(p_1, \ldots p_n; p_1^*, \ldots p_n^*) - \bar{x}_n. \qquad (4.1)$$

A state of this system is a particular configuration of $p_1, \ldots p_n, p_1^*, \ldots p_n^*$, since any choice of these $2n$ prices yields a particular level of excess demand for the n goods, and thus a particular change in the price set if price change in any market depends on the excess demand in that market. In short, there

[1] Intertemporal problems abound; for example, it must be assumed that traders can issue notes for one period which must be redeemed. With certainty assumptions, the two period budget constraint is easy to develop. With uncertainty, this is very difficult [27, 9].

are now $2n$ state variables; the n current prices and the n currently held expectations of future prices.

In order to determine an equilibrium it ought to be apparent that some other feature must be added to system 4.1, for there are 'n equations' with '$2n$ unknowns'. The escape from this dilemma is simple. Suppose that the current price of good i is different from the currently held expectation of the price of good i; say that $p_i^* < p_i$. What might happen? Certainly if one wanted to model concrete individual behaviour, one might wish to suppose that traders would modify their expectations in view of current experience, so that if $p_i^* < p_i$, p_i^* would rise. This simple mechanism, known as *adaptive expectations*, states that expected prices increase (decrease) if the current price is greater (lower) than the current expectation of the future price.[1]

Under what circumstances will an equilibrium exist? It must be the case that the state of the system remains unchanged over time, but a state of the system is the set of current *and* expected prices. Current prices change depending on excess demand, and expected prices change depending on the difference between current and expected prices. Thus an equilibrium state is a vector $(p_1, \ldots p_n; p_1^*, \ldots p_n^*)$ such that

$$E_1 = D_1(p_1, p_2, \ldots p_n; p_1^*, \ldots p_n^*) - \bar{x}_1 = 0$$
$$E_2 = D_2(p_1, p_2, \ldots p_n; p_1^*, \ldots p_n^*) - \bar{x}_2 = 0$$
$$\vdots$$
$$E_n = D_n(p_1, p_2, \ldots p_n; p_1^*, \ldots p_n^*) - \bar{x}_n = 0$$
$$p_1 = p_1^*$$
$$p_2 = p_2^*$$
$$\vdots$$
$$p_n = p_n^*. \tag{4.2}$$

Intuitively, an equilibrium position is one in which supply equals demand in all markets, *and* current prices are expected to prevail in all markets.

Does an equilibrium position exist? It is easy to see that an equilibrium will exist if and only if an equilibrium exists for the system without expectations, since setting $p_1 = p_1^*, p_2 = p_2^*, \ldots p_n = p_n^*$ reduces system 4.2 to the system of Chapter 2 (recalling the homogeneity of the demand functions). The same assumptions which entailed existence of equilibrium for the

[1] What is ruled out is behaviour like 'if $p_i > p_i^*$, p_i is out of line and p_i^* should be even lower'.

exchange model without expectations suffice when adaptive expectations are introduced [27, 9].

STABILITY

The question of stability is a bit more complicated. Intuitively, given a disequilibrium state $(p_1, \ldots p_n; p_1^*, \ldots p_u^*)$, are the rules which govern change such as to move that state closer to equilibrium over time? The problem is that there are two different kinds of dynamic mechanisms at work; the first, the tatonnement, changes current prices, while the second, adaptive expectations, moves currently held expectations of future prices.

In order to provide some justification for the major theorem of this section, consider a simple example involving a single price: let p^* denote the expectations of period $t + 1$ price currently held in period t, and let p be the actual price in period t. Adaptive expectations then entail

$$\frac{d}{dt}(p^*) = k(p - p^*) \text{ where } k > 0.[1] \qquad (4.3)$$

Thus if $p > p^*$, p^* increases, and if $p < p^*$, p^* decreases. If p is a given number, then the adaptive expectations mechanism forces expected price closer to actual; all prices converge on equilibrium.

The point to notice is that adaptive expectations is a stable mechanism, so that the stability of the system 4.2 depends *only* on the stability of the usual tatonnement mechanism. But since stability conditions have already been established for the usual system, it only remains to link the expectations with the excess demand functions.

Recall that gross substitutability was crucial in the non-expectations case. If it is assumed, then, that all future goods are gross substitutes for all present goods[2] (so that $\delta E_i / \delta p_j^* > 0$ for all i, j) then *the exchange model with adaptive expectations is stable if and only if the model is stable when expectations are static,* (that is, they do not change) [27, 9].

In short, given a stable expectationless general equilibrium

---

[1] Solving this for fixed p shows that p^* is a weighted average of the p, so if p converges so does p^*, and conversely.

[2] This is probably less objectionable than the usual assumption that all current goods are gross substitutes.

model of exchange, and adding expected prices and adaptive expectations mechanisms, there is no loss in stability. The extension of the basic model to include expectations involves no loss of explanatory power; the theorems are robust with respect to expectations of future prices held with confidence.[1]

PRODUCTION

A real objection to the use of exchange models is that serious economic problems involve decisions to produce, as well as decisions to consume, fixed stocks of commodities. The standard model of Chapter 2 attempted to analyse consumption behaviour in the context of a fully interrelated system. It is now time to see whether a similar treatment of production can be developed and integrated into the general equilibrium model [28].

It will be recalled that the Walrasian system required excess demand functions for all commodities; these functions were the difference between demand and supply. Supply up to now was taken to be fixed, so excess demand, and the system, depended only on demand or consumer choice. There is thus a need to develop a production theory to support supply choices which enter the general equilibrium system as supply functions. There can be no hope of generality until this is done.

The important concept which must be introduced is that of a *production set* for a given firm. For any firm defined here as an output producing unit, it is assumed that the firm can choose a combination of inputs and outputs. If inputs are written as negative outputs, the case of one input (say labour) and one output (say corn) would be written as a pair of numbers. If seven labour units were needed to produce three bushels of corn, the point $(-7, 3)$ would represent one feasible point in the firm's production set [28, 29].

The set of all technologically feasible productions for a firm constitute the firm's set. The shaded area Y_i represent the production set for firm i in Fig. 11.

Various assumptions must be made about the production set in order to guarantee the existence of supply functions,

[1] It can be shown, however, that if the expectations are not held with certainty, so that a random error may occur in the formation of expectations, the stability of the expectationless system no longer entails stability of the system with expectations [27].

much as assumptions about consumer preferences were needed to ensure regular demand functions.

It is assumed, usually, that (0,0) is in the production set, so the firm always has the option of doing nothing at all. It is also assumed that the production set does not intersect the non-negative quadrant except at the origin; in other words,

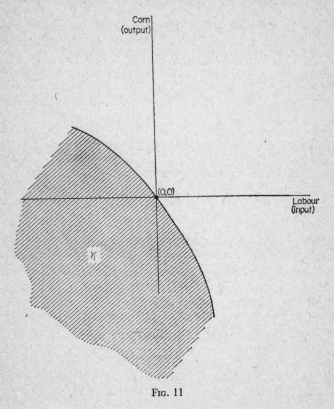

Fig. 11

some inputs must be used in order to obtain a positive output. It is further assumed that the negative quadrant is in Y_i; this 'free disposal' assumption says that the firm can get rid of outputs without using up inputs. Finally, it is assumed that Y_i is convex for each firm i, an assumption which essentially ensures diminishing returns and decreasing returns to scale.

Now just as a consumer was assumed to maximise utility subject to a budget constraint, the producer will be supposed to maximise profits, or net income, subject to the constraint that the chosen output must lie on or inside the production

46

set. (Profits are computed with a given (exogeneous) factor and product prices.)

It is not difficult to see that for different output prices the quantity of the output that will be produced will change; this relationship is the supply curve, so supply quantities will depend on output price and all input prices. Under the assumptions laid out above for the production set, all supply curves will slope upward so all theorems about the existence of a competitive equilibrium remain valid in the production case.[1] Further, the stability theorems derived from assumptions like gross substitutability continue to hold [29].

LIMITATIONS OF THE PRODUCTION MODEL

The incorporation of production into the general equilibrium model seems quick and painless. A few innocuous looking assumptions seem to ensure that a competitive equilibrium price vector exists, and that a tatonnement price adjustment mechanism will ensure stability of that equilibrium vector. Before proceeding to extend this model to phrase macro-economic questions, consider some of its limitations.

Viewing the production set for a firm as independent of the choices made by other firms entails that there are no external economies or diseconomies. Since a large part of governments' role in economic affairs depends on the existence of diseconomies, it may be difficult to envisage policies about pollution, congestion, crime, etc. ever being discussed in the context of this standard general equilibrium system.

Convexity of the production set, which implies decreasing returns to scale, rules out any discussion of monopoly, oligopoly, barriers to entry of new firms, unionisation in the labour market, patents, information imperfections in any factor or product market, etc. It may be that any or all of these phenomena are uninteresting (which is unlikely) or unimportant for macro-economics (which is even more unlikely). The point, however, is that none of these questions can even be phrased in the context of the only comprehensive general equilibrium system that economists have been able to analyse [30].

Profit maximisation as an assumption also introduces an unreal element into the discussion. As an hypothesis it is merely

[1] A proof of this is non-trivial; see [9, 29]

fruitful or unfruitful. Yet it is on occasion useful to speak of various problems that are swept away by this catch-all. For example, who is it within the firm that maximises profit? Since all employees maximise utility subject to their budget constraints, the profit maximising entrepreneur must actually be just another undifferentiated worker whose own labour he hires to produce outputs of commodities [31].

And finally, the model assumes a stock of workers and equipment that is always fully employed.

A PRELIMINARY SUMMARY

The first four chapters provide an overview of the kind of general equilibrium system used in economics to elucidate the role of the price system in mediating between conflicting decisions of consumers and producers when all their actions are interrelated. Under various restrictions it has been shown that a competitive equilibrium price vector exists, is stable, and possesses some rudimentary social welfare implications.

Yet general equilibrium theory as a type of general systems analysis ought to provide various linkages with the aggregative structure of macroeconomic theory as well as to the disaggregative structure of microeconomic analysis.

The preceding chapters have been built up by abstracting from individual decisions. It is now time to survey some attempts to use the general equilibrium system as a lynchpin of macroeconomics; logic and tradition dictate that this route should be via monetary theory since it is the distinction between barter and monetary economies that gives macroeconomics its flavour [32, 33].

5 Money and General Equilibrium

'The importance of money essentially flows from its being a link between the present and the future.' (J. M. Keynes)

For many years the division between microeconomics and macroeconomics has been detailed and condemned by economists, while the link between the two, general equilibrium theory, has suffered from a curious form of neglect. Although it has been well understood that macroeconomic structures could be 'aggregated up' from general systems models, this insight remained of purely academic interest as long as the general models remained so unwordly; concern for axiomatisation of production relations in a timeless barter world, while not uninteresting, cannot be the hallmark of a worldview flexible enough to cope with problems of inflation or involuntary unemployment.

Yet it is to the credit of various general equilibrium theorists that such important concerns were never so far from their analytic work that they ignored completely the macro implications of their models. From Walras on, there has been an attempt to grapple with the salient features of a monetary economy. If it is true, as many observe, that time and money are essential characteristics of actual economic systems, general equilibrium theory cannot be faulted for its inattention to these details, though its meagre and sometimes confusing conclusions can be derided.

In this chapter several monetary general equilibrium models will be introduced; their assumptions and importance will differ greatly, but they do provide a view of what a unified economic theory might be like. Since the subject is one of great current controversy, only some schematic outlines can be given here; the last chapter will report on some of the new directions that general equilibrium theorists are taking.

As Samuelson notes, the modern theorist who tries to reconstruct how the classical general equilibrium model dealt with money is 'in the position of a man who, looking for a jackass, must say to himself, "If I were a jackass, where would I go?" ' [34].

The starting point of such an exercise must be the Walrasian model of Chapter 2. It will be recalled that the system could be reduced to

$$E_i(p_1, \ldots p_n) = 0; \quad i = 1,2, \ldots n \qquad (5.1)$$

or n excess demand functions of the n commodity prices, when system 5.1 was in equilibrium. This system, which contained one dependent equation, determined $n-1$ relative prices so that if good n were chosen as the numeraire whose price was given, all prices could be expressed in terms of the numeraire as $p_1/p_n, p_2/p_n, \ldots p_{n-1}/p_n$. The system of 'real' or market equations determined real or relative prices. One could not ask for a determination of the absolute level of prices since a doubling, or halving, of all relative prices left system 5.1 unchanged.

How then does the price level, or the level of absolute prices, get determined? Clearly this is a macroeconomic question of some importance.

On one view of the classical system, the level of absolute prices was determined by the equation of exchange. Thus if M is the money supply, and V a known behavioural constant, $\sum_{i=1}^{n} p_i q_i = MV$ added another equation to system 5.1, an independent equation. It can be seen that a doubling of the money supply would double all absolute prices but leave relative prices unchanged since they were determined by excess demand, or the supply and demand for real commodities. There is a sort of dichotomy present: real factors determine relative prices, and monetary factors determine the absolute price level.

It is well to note that no classical author, Walras for example, actually believed that money had no 'real' as opposed to monetary effect. In their various writings they showed a clear awareness that money was intertwined in a myriad of ways with real economic activity. Still, the general equilibrium system with its dichotomy could be considered an ideal case against which actual events could be compared.

Yet there is more to the matter, for the system obtained from 5.1 and the equation of exchange (EOE) is an anomaly; the first part is behavioural, while the second is an identity. To rectify this, and to cast the classical system in its clearest form, rewrite the EOE as

$$M = \frac{1}{V} \Sigma p_i q_i \qquad (5.2)$$

If the left side represents the supply of money, and the right is the demand for money, the excess demand for money would be given by

$$\left(\frac{1}{V} \underset{i}{\Sigma} p_i q_i - M \right)$$

For given V, the excess demand for money depends on all money prices *and* the quantity of money, and since the goods quantities demanded were homogeneous of degree zero in money prices, excess demand for money is homogeneous of degree one in money prices and the quantity of money (i.e. if all prices and the quantity of money double, excess demand for money doubles).

The classical system with money introduced thus consists of n dependent equations for excess demand in the goods markets, and one equation for excess demand for money, where the former are homogeneous of degree zero in money prices and the latter is homogeneous of degree one in money prices and the quantity of money.

THE NEOCLASSICAL SYNTHESIS

What is the effect of assuming that a positive or negative excess demand for money can exist? Considering consumers, a demand for money is a plan to carry cash balances to make future purchases. Thus an excess demand for money is identically equal to an excess supply of goods and services. Yet the excess demand for money from ($\frac{1}{V} \Sigma p_i q_i - M$) is homogeneous of degree one in money prices *and* the quantity of money, while the excess supply of goods is homogeneous of degree one in money prices only. This contradiction is certainly unsatisfactory [35].

The challenge to reconstitute the classical general equilibrium

51

system with money introduced in a consistent manner was taken up by Lange [36] and Patinkin [37]. It is the latter's work which has given form to almost all of the present discussions, and although his analysis is too lengthy to be detailed here, an outline of his neoclassical synthesis[1] can be given.

If the problem for the classical system is rooted in the fact that the money stock appears nowhere in the various commodity excess demands, it might seem a simple matter to make demand quantities depend not only on money prices but the quantity of money. Yet creating another argument in the market demand functions is a non-trivial emendation since the form of those functions depends crucially on the choice behaviour of individuals. Patinkin's chief contribution was to show that individual demands to hold goods could be integrated with the real money balances that individuals desire to hold (as a solution to the intertemporal choice problem) in a consistent manner. Thus if $P = \sum_{i=1}^{n} w_i p_i$ is the price level, a weighted average of money prices p_i with given weights w_i, then P is homogeneous of degree one in money prices.

If M is the given quantity of money, Patinkin's analysis yields $n+1$ excess demand equations of the form

$$E_1 = E_1 \left(\frac{p_1}{P}, \frac{p_2}{P}, \ldots \frac{p_n}{P}, \frac{M}{P} \right)$$

$$\vdots$$

$$E_n = E_n \left(\frac{p_1}{P}, \frac{p_2}{P}, \ldots \frac{p_n}{P}, \frac{M}{P} \right)$$

$$E_{n+1} = M^d \left(\frac{p_1}{P}, \ldots \frac{p_n}{P}, \frac{M}{P} \right) - \frac{M}{P} \qquad (5.3)$$

The first n of these equations pertain to the goods markets, and excess demand for goods depends on the n *relative* prices and *real* (deflated) money balances. The $(n+1)$st market is for money, and excess demand for real money balances is the difference between demand, dependent on relative prices and real money balances, and supply.

Since a supply of goods is a demand for money and vice versa, Walras' Law (from the hidden budget constraints)

[1] 'Neoclassical synthesis' means different things to different economists. Here it is taken to mean the marriage of modern monetary theory to the 'classical' (meaning Walrasian) general equilibrium (or value) theory.

shows that one market is dependent on the others. (With the equation for the price level, setting E_1 through E_{n+1} equal to zero gives $n+2$ equations in the $n+1$ variables $(p_1/P, p_2/P, \ldots M/P)$. With the money market, say, eliminated, there is a determinate system in which the excess demand for money still appears in the form of an excess supply of commodities. More important, however, real money balances enter all excess demands which are, in consequence, homogeneous of degree zero in money prices *and* the quantity of money.

Does an equilibrium price vector exist for system 5.3? Without going too deeply into the matter here, if money enters the demand functions in a smooth way so that the demand functions are differentiable, as Patinkin assumes, a unique equilibrium exists, and the tatonnement mechanism which changes prices in the direction of excess demand can be used to show that the equilibrium is a stable one.

It is an interesting fact that even without the EOE, an increase in the quantity of money can be shown, in 5.3, to lead to an increase in the price level but to no change at all in relative prices. For if (p_i, P) is an equilibrium, and M changes to aM, the new solution is (ap_i, aP). It is this completely classical proposition, derived without using the EOE, that gives the neoclassical system its flavour.

THE TAMING OF KEYNES

Money supplies do not just happen; they are debt created by the government (outside money) and the market participants through financial intermediaries (inside money). It is necessary then to specify further the particular markets in system 5.3 beyond the crude 'commodity' and 'money' market split. Patinkin introduces markets for consumer goods, capital goods, intermediary inputs, factor services (labour mostly), bonds, and money, and specifies the excess demands which arise from the choices and budget constraints in each of the markets. In outline, 5.3 continues to structure the analysis so that one market is dependent in the full general equilibrium system [35, 37].

On some interpretations of the *General Theory*, Keynes was supposed to have demonstrated the possibility of involuntary unemployment, or disequilibrium in the labour market, concurrent with equilibrium in the goods markets and money markets. In this view, given a neoclassical general equilibrium framework for the Keynesian system, the first $n-1$ markets are in equilibrium while the labour market is not. Yet from the Patinkin system this is impossible if prices (and wages or factor prices) are flexible, since Walras' Law ensures that equilibrium in the first $n-1$ markets entails equilibrium in the nth. Consequently Keynesian unemployment must be a result of money wage rigidity in the labour market or, alternatively, labour must be irrational and 'off' its supply curve.

Speaking roughly, from such a perspective the Keynesian contribution to pure theory comes to be hardly worth even a footnote, being merely an investigation of a special case. As Leijonhufvud points out [6], theoretical honours were given to the neoclassicals while it was granted that the 'special case' was of great practical importance for public policy. Keynes' *General Theory*, on such a view, was neither 'general' nor a 'theory'.

THE KEYNESIAN COUNTERREVOLUTION

The picture of the Keynesian revolution which emerges from the neoclassical synthesis has not been universally accepted. Various writers, including those U.K. economists closest to Keynes like Kahn, Robinson, Kaldor, and Harrod, have steadfastly refused to accept Keynes' contribution as a special case: Shackle [38], Weintraub [17], Davidson [33] and others have clearly understood the reasons why the neoclassical prism distorts the Keynesian vision.

It has been a minor triumph of general equilibrium theory, however abstract and rarefied as it may seem, that it has reconstituted the Keynesian revolution and breathed life into those issues of pure theory with which Keynes grappled but which the neoclassicals ignored.

It is only in recent years, perhaps, that general equilibrium theory can be said to have come of age and taken a place in the tool-kit economists use to phrase and answer questions of practical import.

An opening round in the controversy was fired by Clower [39] and Hahn [40]. The latter pointed out that in order to infer the existence of an equilibrium price vector in Patinkin's system a peculiar assumption was needed to ensure that there was a positive demand for money at all positive values of money, and this Hahn argued really begged the entire existence problem. Meanwhile Clower was able to show that the budget constraints which were used to derive the supply curves for factor services and commodity demands (and thus factor derived demands) were of a very strange nature. Clower reintroduced the distinction between effective demands for goods, demands based on *realised* income, and notional demands which were based on incomes *anticipated* by consumers. Only with full employment, Clower argued, would these coincide. More frequently, the signals transmitted by effective demands were incorrect since realised income might fall short of anticipated income, so a temporary excess supply of goods could lead to an excess supply of labour, or unemployment. As expectations were modified, the excess supply of goods would be absorbed and the goods markets could be in equilibrium with unemployment present.

Clower's contribution forced awareness of the dynamic or disequilibrium processes at the heart of the monetary general equilibrium model. Contracts or agreements made in money terms constrain the tatonnement process by which markets adjust. The presence of transactions costs, and trade out of equilibrium, mean that money is not just another commodity, since money and goods trade against one another, but goods do not trade directly against goods.

Leijonhufvud [32] placed a number of these issues in their appropriate context. As seen in Chapter 2, the price system conveys information to the market participants in such a manner that resources are allocated in an optimal fashion. Price movements are signals indicating excess demand or supply for goods and services. The assumptions of this model, of a barter economy, included 'fixed income' of the traders. In a production world, like that of Chapter 4, individual choices were still constrained by given budgets.

The neoclassical demand for money, which analyses the desire to carry cash balances forward to make purchases tomorrow as well as today, assumes that the market participants can actually decide today on their future purchase pattern. That is, they correctly foresee future tastes and income so that even if they have expectations, those expectations are held with confidence. To Leijonhufvud, this view of the world is one which Keynes rejected.

Keynes, it is argued, believed that individuals do hold

55

money as a store of wealth. This fact, though, cannot be reconciled with any view of an economic system which operates, as the neoclassical models do, without uncertainty.[1] For Keynes stated that '. . . partly on reasonable and partly on instinctive grounds, our desire to hold money as a store of wealth is a barometer of the degree of our distrust of our own calculations and conventions concerning the future . . . the significance of this characteristic of money has usually been overlooked' [48, p. 216].

For Leijonhufvud, then, fundamental uncertainty about the future enters into the choice between money and capital goods for producers, and money and consumer goods for consumers. To the extent that these choices are not made with confidence, the price signals that reflect the choices may convey misleading information, and this is at the heart of the resource allocation failure, labour unemployment, that concerned Keynes and that must characterise any Keynesian system.

On this view of Keynes, the neoclassical system never really analyses a monetary economy in which money has asset properties; instead such a system assumes that the insights of a barter economy 'carry over' to actual economies.

The problem cannot at this time be called 'settled'. So far, no general equilibrium system has been developed that fully respects the singular set of arrangements under which transactions occur in a monetary economy, though it is only such a system that could be used to evaluate macroeconomic arguments.

[1] A state of the world is 'risky' if a probability can be attached to its occurrence. The state is 'uncertain' if no such probability can be attached with confidence.

6 Recent Developments and New Directions

In this final chapter a number of issues, mentioned briefly before, will be outlined in more detail since they are both current and unsettled. The work that is being done today in general equilibrium theory rests, as it must, on past insights; yet as the last chapter showed such models have been only partially useful in grappling with some major problems of interest to economists. It may be relevant then to survey some current research, for out of today's 'new directions' may come tomorrow's 'standard treatment'.

GENERAL SYSTEMS THEORY

Perhaps the most informed, dogged, and argumentative attack on the standard general equilibrium model to appear recently is that of J. Kornai in his book *Anti-Equilibrium* [3]. Kornai, an expert in planning models for centralised economies, points out in the clearest terms just how narrow an analytic description the Walrasian system is.

As noted in Chapter 1, a general systems theory, if it were used in economics, would hardly take as its domain the market or price system alone. Control mechanisms and control points, information networks, message flows, decision rules, hierarchical organisation of the entire system, adaptability and survival, all would necessarily appear in a complete systems view of an economy. Kornai argues that the Walrasian scheme, while once a useful abstraction, does not describe anything of interest; as a first approximation it had some value, but economists forgot that it was only a first step.

Without evaluating this argument, it should be recognised that Clower and Leijonhufvud can be said to provide Kornai with some support, since they have been concerned with the failure of price signals to convey the proper information in a monetised general equilibrium structure of the neoclassical type. Unemployment, in their view of Keynes, is an information problem inherent in the way individuals make decisions to purchase commodities. Kornai is thus correct in suggesting that these problems must be faced; his model, however, is probably too cumbersome for many economists to do more than agree with his diagnosis.

Some related work has been done by D. Katzner [41] on general systems theory. Katzner argues that one of the major barriers to the formulation of a full systems type of general equilibrium theory, not just in economics but also in sociology, political science, etc., is the mistaken belief that the variables which enter these systems must be measurable. Clearly the choice that economists made in selecting prices as the basic state variables was a reflection of the desire to work with objects that could be added, multiplied, compared, and otherwise manipulated by the rules of arithmetic. If many economists do not feel comfortable using phrases like 'degree of monopoly power' it may be because they feel it is not quantifiable.

What Katzner has pointed out, however, is that general equilibrium theory can work with non-measurable variables. That is, systems concepts like state variable, equilibrium, parameter, stability, etc. do not depend on the fact that state variables take values in a subset of real numbers: they can just as easily have values in abstract sets. It is thus meaningful to set up models which have 'quality of life' as a variable. Certainly the aridity of having only price variables in a general equilibrium model is as unnecessary as it may be misleading.

THE EXCHANGE SYSTEM

The new approach to the exchange model using the core of an economy as the equilibrium concept has been actively pursued. Hildenbrand [42] has been able to unify the finite and continuum of traders' models by showing that both could be considered special cases of a more general representation.

Shitovitz [43] has shown that it is possible to create a model in which some of the traders are large in relation to others; some of his results suggest that a unified oligopoly–competition general equilibrium model might be attainable; at the present there is no satisfactory general equilibrium model with imperfectly competitive elements.

Related to this problem is the question of economic power, since one way of modelling monopolistic elements is by allowing certain traders more power than others. Work by Shapley and Milnor [44] has attempted to analyse the kinds of solutions which arise in a bargaining game, not unlike the exchange game, when some players are large in relation to many small undifferentiated players.

Starrett has attempted to introduce various external effects [45] in general equilibrium models. This kind of extension of the system is needed if practical issues are to be analysed in a systematic fashion.

NON-TATONNEMENT PROCESSES

For a number of years there has been a concern that the central dynamic mechanism of general equilibrium theory, the tatonnement, is an inadequate tool to unravel the complicated issues which arise in monetised models. For example, whose behaviour is modelled by the rule 'price moves in the direction of excess demand'? One can only posit an artificial auctioneer who adjusts price on the basis of information the traders provide him (by buy and sell orders) as he calls out various price configurations.

F. Fisher has approached this problem [46] by working with a barter model incorporating two non-standard features: (1) money has a medium-of-exchange role, but only excess demands which have money to back them up are assumed to affect prices; and (2) certain individuals are 'dealers' in every non-money commodity, and they set prices in response to buy or sell orders. In this framework, customers (non-dealers) search among dealers to find the 'best buy', so price movement depends on the various search procedures. This sort of model resembles the Clower treatment (recall 'effective demands' and transactions rules).

Using various technical assumptions Fisher proves a stability theorem for this disequilibrium process, but remarks that 'once we abandon the fictitious auctioneer, the problem becomes richer. In some ways, that richness leads to greater difficulty . . . .' Certainly more work will be done along these lines.

UNCERTAINTY

The extension of the traditional Walrasian model to a world in which the future is uncertain is surely a step in the direction of increased applicability of the system, since the role of money as an asset cannot be seen without an intertemporal decision calculus.

The theorist most responsible for interest in these questions is R. Radner [47], who in various papers has sought to extend the neoclassical system by introducing uncertainty. '. . . if decision makers receive information about each other's behaviour as well as about the environment, then this introduces a type of externality (interdependence) among their decision rules. This type of externality has the result that

59

decision makers must take account of uncertainty about each other's behaviour as well as about the environment.' Radner notes that only the latter type of uncertainty is able to be modelled by the standard theory of competitive equilibrium.

His approach is to divide actions into decisions controlled by economic agents and environmental variables which are uncontrolled. A specification of the environment is a *state of nature,* and agents are assumed to have information about the states of nature, though different agents may have different information. Choices are made by the producers and consumers based on their estimation of the likelihood that certain states will prevail, so attitudes towards risk play an important part in Radner's model. He concludes that '. . . if economic decision makers are uncertain about the environment, and if their information is about the environment, then even if they have different information, a once-and-for-all futures market in conditional contracts can achieve an optimum allocation of resources, relative to the given structure of information.' This pessimistic conclusion entails, however, that the important problems of money and liquidity probably cannot be handled in the context of an extended classical model.

TRADE-OUT-OF-EQUILIBRIUM

If the tatonnement is unrealistic, and information about others' behaviour is lacking but necessary to make once-and-for-all optimum decisions, it is of interest to investigate various piecemeal or step-by-step strategies for trading. One such process, of a gradient sort, has been explored by Graham and Weintraub [24].

Consider the exchange problem which arises when various not necessarily similar individuals have endowments of several commodities. Is the initial allocation Pareto-optimal? If it is, no trade would take place under circumstances of perfect costless information, since in any exchange at least one of the parties would be made worse off, so he would not have agreed to the trade.

Thus suppose the original allocation is not Pareto-optimal. Then there exists at least one coalition of traders that could form, redistribute their holdings, and make all members of that coalition better off. With costless information, if there are any gains-from-trade to be captured, then there is a nonzero probability that some such gain will be captured; it can be shown, then, that at least one coalition will form and trade and capture some (but perhaps not all) of the possible gain.

Consider the resulting allocation which consists of the new redistribution to the coalition and the initial holdings of the rest of the traders. If this is Pareto-optimal, no new trading results. If it is not, iterate the above argument. It can be shown that this process converges on a Pareto-optimal allocation that is a core allocation with respect to the most recent endowment, and thus the price vectors implicit in any sequence of such exchanges converge on an equilibrium price vector which supports an optimal allocation.

An interesting feature of this process is that transactions costs can be built into the adjustment rules so that the resulting allocation can be compared to the standard distribution.

Further, the individual decision to enter a trading coalition can be based on imperfect information, or it may be costly to join a coalition even if no trade takes place. This feature of information costs recalls Radner's view of the interdependence of trader's strategies. It is possible that such an approach, resembling Fisher's but phrased in game-theoretic terms, could be used to extend the class of disequilibrium processes economists study since a variety of institutional constraints could be introduced to restrict the choice behaviour implicit in coalition formation.

A CONCLUDING NOTE

The past decade has been a period of great ferment in economic theory, though the mathematisation of the subject has partially concealed the uproar from public view. General equilibrium theory, situated in the middle ground between microeconomics and macroeconomics, has both reflected and induced changes in the larger corpus of economic analysis. A reconstitution of the 'standard model' has been taking place although this fact has scarcely been recognised outside the specialised and mathematically sophisticated readership of various theoretical journals. If the past history of economics is a guide, however, spillover effects can be expected to occur with increasing frequency in the next few years, to the enrichment of discussion in all areas of economic theory.

Bibliography

[1] L. von Bertalanffy, *General System Theory* (George Braziller, New York, 1968).

[2] M. D. Mesarovic (ed.), *Views on General Systems Theory* (Wiley, New York, 1964).

[3] J. Kornai, *Anti-Equilibrium* (American Elsevier, New York, 1971).

[4] K. Boulding, *Beyond Economics, Essays on Society, Religion and Ethics* (University of Michigan Press, 1968).

[5] B. Hansen, *General Equilibrium Systems* (McGraw-Hill, New York 1970).

[6] A. Leijonhufvud, *Keynes and the Classics* (Institute of Economic Affairs, London, 1969).

[7] K. Arrow, 'The Organization of Economic Activity' in *Frontiers of Quantitative Economics*, ed. M. Intriligator, (North-Holland, Amsterdam, 1970).

[8] R. Clower (ed.), *Readings in Monetary Theory* (Penguin, Harmondsworth, 1970).

[9] K. Arrow and F. Hahn, *General Competitive Analysis* (Oliver & Boyd, Edinburgh, 1971).

[10] J. Robinson, *Economic Heresies* (Macmillan, London, 1971).

[11] V. Walsh, *Introduction to Contemporary Micreoconomics* (McGraw-Hill, New York, 1970).

[12] I. N. Herstein and J. Milnor, 'An Axiomatic Approach to Measurable Utility' *Econometrica*, 21 (1953).

[13] R. G. D. Allen, *Mathematical Economics* (Macmillan, London, 1956).

[14] S. Weintraub, *Intermediate Price Theory* (Chilton, Philadelphia, 1964).

[15] T. Negishi, 'Stability of a Competitive Economy', *Econometrica*, 30 (1962).

[16] F. Hahn, 'Some Adjustment Problems', *Econometrica*, 39 (1970).

[17] S. Weintraub, *An Approach to the Theory of Income Distribution* (Chilton, Philadelphia, 1958).

[18] P. Newman, *The Theory of Exchange* (Prentice-Hall, Englewood Cliffs, 1965).

[19] G. Owen, *Game Theory* (Saunders, Philadelphia, 1969).

[20] M. Shubik, 'Edgeworth Market Games', in *Contributions to the Theory of Games*, ed. R. D. Luce and A. W. Tucker, vol. 4, Annals of Mathematics Studies No. 40 (Princeton University Press, 1959).

[21] G. Debreu and H. Scarf, 'A Limit Theorem on the Core of an Economy', *International Economic Review* (Sep 1963).

[22] R. Aumann, 'Markets with a Continuum of Traders', *Econometrica*, 32 (1964).

[23] F. Y. Edgeworth, *Mathematical Psychics* (Kegan Paul, London, 1881; reprinted by Kelly & Millman, New York, 1954).

[24] D. A. Graham and E. R. Weintraub, 'On Convergence to Pareto Optimal Allocations' (unpublished).

[25] D. A. Graham, E. Jacobson and E. R. Weintraub, 'Transactions Costs and Convergence of a Trade-Out-of-Equilibrium Adjustment Process', *International Economic Review* (June 1972).

[26] J. M. Keynes, *The General Theory of Employment, Interest, and Money* (Macmillan, London, 1936).

[27] S. Turnovsky and E. R. Weintraub, 'Stochastic Stability of a General Equilibrium System under Adaptive Expectations', *International Economic Review* (Feb 1971).

[28] T. C. Koopmans, (ed.), *Activity Analysis of Allocation and Production* (Wiley, New York, 1951).

[29] J. Quirk, and R. Saposnik, *Introduction to General Equilibrium Theory and Welfare Economics* (McGraw-Hill, New York, 1968).

[30] M. Shubik, 'A Curmudgeon's Guide to Microeconomics' *Journal of Economic Literature* (June 1970).

[31] O. E. Williamson, *The Economics of Discretionary Behavior: Managerial Objectives in a Theory of the Firm* (Prentice-Hall, New Jersey, 1964).

[32] A. Leijonhufvud, *On Keynesian Economics and the Economics of Keynes* (Oxford University Press, London, 1968).

[33] P. Davidson, *Money in the Real World* (Macmillan, London, 1972).

[34] P. A. Samuelson, 'What Classical and Neo-Classical Monetary Theory Really Was', *Canadian Journal of Economics* (1968).

[35] B. Hansen, *A Survey of General Equilibrium Systems* (McGraw-Hill, New York, 1970).

[36] O. Lange, *Price Flexibility and Employment* (Principia, Bloomington, Indiana, 1945).

[37] D. Patinkin, *Money, Interest, and Prices*, 2nd edition (Harper & Row, New York, 1965).

[38] G. L. S. Shackle, *The Years of High Theory* (Cambridge University Press, 1967).

[39] R. W. Clower, 'The Keynesian Counter-revolution: A Theoretical Appraisal', in *The Theory of Interest Rates*, ed. F. Hahn and F. Brechling (Macmillan, London, 1965).

[40] F. Hahn, 'On Some Problems of Proving the Existence of and Equilibrium in a Monetary Economy', in Hahn and Brechling (see [39]).

[41] D. Katzner, *Analysis Without Measurement* (unpublished).

[42] W. Hildenbrand, 'On Economies with Many Agents', *Journal of Economic Theory* (June 1970).

[43] B. Shitovitz, 'Oligopoly in Markets with a Continuum of Traders', *Econometrica* (forthcoming).

[44] L. Shapley and J. Milnor, 'Values of Large Games, II: Oceanic Games', RAND Working Paper RM2649 (Feb 1961).

[45] D. Starret, 'Fundamental Nonconvexities in the Theory of Externalities', *Journal of Economic Theory* (Apr 1972).

[46] F. Fisher, 'On Price Adjustment Without an Auctioneer', *Review of Economic Studies* (Jan 1972).

[47] R. Radner, 'Competitive Equilibrium Under Uncertainty', *Econometrica* (Jan 1968).

[48] J. M. Keynes, 'The General Theory of Employment', *Quarterly Journal of Economics* (Feb 1937).